Book of Love
" HIM "

Brandy Hadnot

INTELLIGENT PUBLISHING

Columbia, MD
https://intelpub.com

Copyright © 2018 by Brandy Hadnot

All rights reserved. Manufactured in the United States of America. No part of this book may be reproduced in any written, electronic, recording, or photocopying form without written permission of the publisher, except by a reviewer, who may quote brief passages in a review. Published by Intelligent Publishing, P. O. Box 809, Columbia, MD 21044. https://intelpub.com.

Cover Design: Intelligent Publishing
Interior Design: Intelligent Publishing
Editors: Lutrish Gundawa

Library of Congress Control Number: 2019941534
Brandy Hadnot
Book of Love: Him
1. Non-Fiction 2. History 3. Romance

ISBN: 978-1-7329425-6-1

Printed in the United States of America

10   9   8   7   6   5   4   3   2   1

DEDICATION

To Those Who Have Given Up on Believing in Or Ever Finding True Love. Don't Give Up. Remember Things Happen When They are Supposed To. True Love Does Exist and True Love Does Prevail. It Will Find You When You Least Expect. You Never Know What Lies Ahead for Your Next Level of Life.

Contents

DEDICATION	3
ACKNOWLEDGMENTS	5
INTRODUCTION	6
CHAPTER ONE - HEAD OVER HEALS	7
CHAPTER TWO - HE SAID YES	11
CHAPTER THREE - I LOST HIM	19
CHAPTER FOUR - CONGRATULATIONS!	22
CHAPTER FIVE – MEMORIES OF HIM	26
CHAPTER SIX - LIFE FOR ME	32
CHAPTER SEVEN - OBEDIENCE IS BETTER THAN SACRIFICE	42
CHAPTER EIGHT – HIM	47
ABOUT THE AUTHOR	55

ACKNOWLEDGEMENTS

Firstly, I Would Like to Thank God for Orchestrating Our True Love Story and For Allowing It to Be Shared to The World.

I Want to Give A Huge Thank You to The Love of My World Mr. D. Reed for Being the Only Boy Who Could Make My Heart Forget Its Own Rhythm. Thank You for Being My Inspiration and My Motivation. Thank You for Your Guidance and For All of Your Patience, Not to Mention All of The Love You Have Shown Me. Thank You for Not Only Believing in Me but For All of The Hard Work You've Dedicated to My Success. You Mean the World to Me and Always Have. Thank You for Showing Me That True Love Does Exist.

Thank You to My Son for Being So Proud and Supportive of Me. Throughout This Time. I Pray That I'm A Good Enough Example to You That Anything Is Achievable in Life.

Thank You to The Editor for Taking the Time to Edit and Give the Best Feedback to Help My Book Become the Best it Could Be.

Thank You to Those Who Gave A Listening Ear During the Early Stages of My Book. I hope that you enjoy the finished product. There Is More to Come from Here. I Look Forward to Giving You More of What You Love to Read.

INTRODUCTION

We all want to believe in real genuine love. We all would like to believe in true soul mates. The majority of us are convinced that we have found our souls mates or long-lost loves. In today's society the idea of love is far and in between. For reasons within society, to include social status, educational background, religion or simply distance, in one way or another some of us have given up hope of ever experiencing such an amazing action of Love or the idea that true love can ever be found. This is the story of how two souls that started out as kids having not known love and its power, finding this type of love and how it will always prevail.

My name is Brandy and I want to take you on the journey with me. I want to share with you my true story and give firsthand accounts that inspired me to share my love story with you. I can prove that true love and its power does exist.

CHAPTER ONE - HEAD OVER HEALS

He was just a regular boy to me. He happened to be the sibling of my best friend. May she rest in peace and shine her Blessings upon He and I.

I'm not sure what it was that triggered my interest but it struck me in a way that my young mind could not comprehend at the time. All I knew was I fell head over heels for a boy who would never and who could never be replaced by another. He was 2 years ahead of me in school, so I never remember us seeing one another in school during junior high years. I would see him on the bus rides home. I remember the crazy looks I would give him because all he did was rap and sing the whole ride home. However, eventually deep down I would really start to adore Him. I became curious about Him and began asking questions about Him from my best friend who, as I mentioned, just so happened to be his sister. Of course, she was somewhat vague in her responses because this was her brother and as siblings, we all would rather watch paint dry than to worry ourselves about the details of what our siblings are up to. So, I understood. However, it did not deter my curiosity.

All I knew was there was something about Him that made my eyes twinkle and my heart yearn for something I could not describe. He became my motivation and my desperation all at once. Being as young as I was, I had no idea how to contain such a dynamic energy that kept pulling me in his direction. This was something that seemed to have developed all on its own. Love had set up shop in my heart and refused to leave and, quite honestly, I didn't want it to leave.

It wasn't long before my classmates and friends began to notice how intrigued I was by this one boy. Although there were a few other boys that did interest me, it wasn't enough to pull me away from what was in my sights. So, everyone just gave up and accepted the fact that I only had eyes for Him. I couldn't wait for my junior high school years to be over because I knew that once I got to high school, I could see Him every day. I was beside myself just thinking of it all. It never occurred to me to think of what to do next if indeed I did get to gain his attention.

I grew up as a preacher's kid or a P.K. as they called us. My life, as a young girl, was lived under very strict responsible rules. My days, depending upon the day of the week, consisted of choir rehearsal, mission, youth meetings during the week, occasional church on Saturdays, and church for sure on Sundays. Yes of course I was raised by very loving parents. They loved me dearly but boys were not a topic I felt welcome to discuss with my parents. My focus was supposed to be on school and church. I did have my home girls as we called each other then, but boys were kept at bay. I also participated in sports, I played volleyball and I was also on the track team. I enjoyed them both, however, nothing could make me quite as joyful and full of happiness as when I saw Him. He was like a breath of fresh flowing air.

Eventually we attended the same church. As teenagers, participating in church and the youth department where very important and considered a must do. I remember being in the choir stand during church singing, when the church doors opened and in walked Him and his family. My heart jumped out of my chest, or at least it felt that way. My adrenalin never rushed so hard, was this really happening. Not long after, He and His family became regular members of the church. I, of course, was glad that my best friend and I now attended the same church but I was ecstatic that I would get to see Him outside of school. We attended youth meeting and youth outings, and every time I would see Him my heart pounded with anticipation. Little did I know this feeling would be with me forever.

CHAPTER TWO - HE SAID YES

By the time I was a freshman in high school, and with a lot ahead of me, I would still find myself in a daze daydreaming of how my life would be like with Him in it. All of my books would be covered with His name on them. It was clear that I was consumed with him, I couldn't get Him out of my mind even if I seriously and willingly tried. This boy had every part of my being dancing to the beat of a drum that he had no idea existed.

One day, my friends and I were in class joking around. Now everyone has that one friend who is very outspoken, and who will say anything and not care who hears or knows it. Well I have one of those friends. As we joked around in class somehow His name came up, and of course I did my usual smile and laugh and became very attentive just at the mentioning of His name. She suggested that since I am so in love with Him and all I do is talk about Him, I should take the chance and ask

Him if he had anyone, meaning was He dating anyone. This was the obvious thing to do considering my feelings for Him but I was so nervous and afraid of being turned down and rejected by the one boy I centered my teenage life around. I couldn't imagine myself approaching Him and risking humiliation. I felt unworthy and not mature enough, not to mention insecure of myself. There were a lot of girls who liked this boy and who I thought stood better chances than I did of dating Him.

In the back of my mind all kinds of thoughts and fears crept in. This could devastate me on a level I did not fully understand yet. As I mentioned boys were not to be my focus. Even knowing all of this I still gave myself permission to the task of finding out. So, I suggested that my friend, who was the bravest and most outspoken one do it for me. Not to my surprise she was very willing to do it. After class she found Him and asked if He was single because she had this Friend who was interested and wanted to talk to Him. I was afraid to approach Him on my own. When we got back in class the word got back to me, I could not believe the response. I was nervous and shocked at the same time. His response was He was not dating anyone and was single.

Now to give you some insight on why I felt unworthy of this handsome, light brown in complexion, cute, dimple faced and very smooth skinned boy. It seemed as though it was the mission of the girls in school to have their chance to date Him. Most of them were of the same graduating class above me and all friends to each other. Some were older than the both of us. Nevertheless, they all wanted the one boy who could walk past me or just be in the same room and make my heart forget its own rhythm. I was consumed by Him from the way he spoke, to the way he walked, the cologne he wore, and especially the way he dressed. This boy had his own swag and non could compete at least from my view. He was so smooth with it he had his own signature; yes, His own signature! He had a way of licking his lips that would melt the chocolate right out of your hands. If you stared hard enough your smile would turn into a grin. He had a way of touching your soul without an invitation, or maybe this all only affected me. I can't ever remember seeing Him mad or upset. He seemed to be so soft and gentle. With all of this in mind I still had my answer and the question became NOW WHAT!

As the class bell was about to rang, I scrambled to gather my thoughts. What would I say? What shouldn't I say? How would I start the conversation? Heck, what if he's not even standing at his usual spot? This spot was right at the center of the main traffic area in the school hallway. My heart was beating out of my chest but I was still smiling. Then the bell rang and I gathered my books and started making my way through the crowd heading in His direction. On the way my girls cheered me on, "You better go get your man girl!" "Don't be scared!" "Try not to smile so much you know how you get when it comes to Him!" "Maybe now we can stop hearing so much about Him. That's all you talk about!" "I'm glad you finally got your chance!" "Don't do nothing I wouldn't do!" Yes, they meant well and were really happy for me, but the rest of the journey had to be mine to take.

As I parted ways and walked down the hallway, I could see Him clear as ever. Yep, standing in that same spot looking so handsome and clean as if He was anticipating seeing me that very moment. He was so filled with charisma and poise that it was hard to tell if he was as nervous as I was. As I approached him, He of course had his friends there with Him. I immediately began smiling and so, did He. There was this I'm glad you came look on his face. Me, on the other hand, was still scrambling for words. I was saying to myself, "Girl you better say something before you mess yourself up!" I walked up and stood next to Him and somehow, I managed to get my words out. I spoke to him by calling him by his last name as I spoke and asked him how He was. He responded with "It's going good," and called me by my last name as well as He spoke to me. Our conversation was naturally flirty mixed with nervousness. My guess is because we had already been around one another through mutual associates, having his sister as my best friend and attending the same church. In one way or another, we had been in one another's presence previously, but this felt different.

The few minutes in between classes and after school seemed to fly by quickly every day. This would be the only time together other than at church. As our dating time went by, we managed to see each other here and there. He came to a few of my games during volleyball season. These times would be as close to dates as we could get. But when I tell you I was so excited but nervous, that would be an understatement. Those turned out to be the best games that I played. I had to show out because my boyfriend was in the building! Like I previously stated He was my motivation so I played hard. We managed to talk a little after my games but it wasn't long before my ride showed up. We would talk over the phone almost daily, which was a for sure thing considering I had my own phone line in my room. The conversations would be of little substance and difficult to have because we never spent enough time together other than between classes at school or at church. This affected our relationship a lot being so young and not understanding much. I know for me that I felt somewhat desperate to show Him that I could be like the other girls He had dated before me. In my mind I had the idea that He had experienced more with them sexually than He and I ever had and maybe this is what kept His attention with them. I had convinced myself that this was the only reason they wanted to date Him because they could not possibly see Him the way I see Him. Sex wasn't my goal. I really wanted to get to know this one boy that I felt so much for. There came a time when He and I had our encounters with one another, but for some reason it never turned out much on a sexual level at least not as much as one would think. Like I stated before, I felt like this was what gained and kept His attention with the others so, a part of me wanted to show and prove to Him that I was a big girl and I could go there. Yet there was an even bigger part of me that was afraid. I knew that once we had sex, it could possibly cause Him to not take me seriously and it would put me in the same category as the girls He had dated.

Having thought about all of this, it was a risk I was willing to take because I was that into Him and was afraid of this being the losing factor in our relationship that was still so new. There was one particular encounter where time was not on our side and we were both very nervous but seemed so sure. He never pressured me one way or the other but as I write our Love story, I again will state it was a risk I was willing to take. It was hard to tell if He completely felt for me what I completely felt for Him; however, He did seem to have some real interest in me, and it didn't feel like it was all sexual. This relieved me so much that I became even more curious about Him. Needless to say, our time never came and felt like I had pressured myself over something that obviously wasn't meant to happen or so I thought at the time.

He and I dated sometime longer, but as time went on, we both began to accept the fact that this was a difficult relationship to have at our age. There were just so many restrictions on one side. Eventually He and I drifted apart like leaves in the ocean. Before I knew it, I and the one boy who could make every part of my being light up just by the mention of His name had already out-lived our journey.

CHAPTER THREE - I LOST HIM

There I was, the girl who was so in Love and had it going on, and now finding myself at the losing end of Love. For the first time ever, I had experienced what real heart break felt like. I felt the pain of what I've heard so many musicians sing about, of what so many poets write about. I had lost Him and I felt that it was for good. This was very difficult to cope with at such a young age. I knew that more freedom for me could be the key to getting the one relationship with the only boy I dreamed of both day and night back to me. I felt this was only going to happen if I went against the house rules and did what most young people who needed more freedom did and sneak out. I thought about it, but at the time I wasn't bold enough to try that because that came with so many consequences if I got caught. I wasn't about to go that route. So, I quickly gave up on that idea.

He and I never verbally broke up but we both knew the underlining reason behind us not being together. I was too disappointed and not to mention just too embarrassed to speak on the issue with Him. It was very painful just to dwell on the thought of our short-lived relationship and how much of my feelings I had invested in Him for so long even before He ever realized it. So, I again had to watch as other girls dated Him. Except this time instead of feeling anxious and curious I felt disappointment, sadness, and pain. I still deeply cared about Him and now He really knew it. However, I don't think He knew just how deep those feelings went. It was more like I had sampled Him and wanted more, but couldn't afford Him. I never dated anyone else during the remaining time of school that I had with Him. Instead I shut out the idea of ever dating anyone else with the hopes of regaining my relationship with Him.

Well this was all in my imagination and remained on my wish list. He and I were still friends and would talk to one another when we would see each other. The conversations were awkward for me because I wanted more than to have friendly conversations with Him. He still was the center of my universe. That had never changed. The good thing about us still talking and interacting was that we were comfortable with one another and no longer nervous. We would still get to have our flirtatious conversations which we both enjoyed as always.

CHAPTER FOUR - CONGRATULATIONS!

Before I knew it, I was counting down the days before He would graduate. We all have been there and know just how excited it all was. There was an excitement about graduation and attending graduation regardless of it being our very own or someone else's. Just the hype and congratulatory spirit of it all is worth attending the ceremony for. Well, for me this one was bitter-sweet and it saddened me even more. The Love of my life would now be leaving for good and I would no longer be able to see His face on a daily basis. How then would I deal with not seeing Him? How would I then know if He was ok? I would miss the scent of His cologne which smelled ooh so good; let's not forget the dimpled smile that could light up a room. How would I even remotely have a chance of possibly being with Him again? What were the odds of us running into one other again once he graduated and moved on in life? All of these things ran through my mind as May 28, 1997 rapidly approached.

I found myself lost and just going through the motions during school. The same girl who once looked forward to school days since junior high school had disappeared. Well the day arrived; it was now His graduation day which strangely felt as if it was my graduation day as well. I would have to finish the remainder of my high school years without Him; something I was clearly not looking forward to.

As I sat and watched His graduation ceremony take place I smiled and went through the motions appearing to be happy. As He walked across the stage to receive His diploma, I cheered for Him. As He sang His graduating class song "I believe I can Fly" written by R&B singer R. Kelly, tears filled my eyes and no matter how hard I tried to hold them back or how quickly I tried to catch them before they fell, the tears were very much real. I disguised my sadness by pretending something was in my eyes.

After the ceremony I made my way down through the crowd to congratulate Him. He had this big smile on His face full of joy, His dimples never failed to disappoint; they always showed up. As we hugged, I congratulated him told him how good he had sounded. The real message, though, was 'congratulations but my heart is broken into pieces.' Somehow, I felt that this would be the last time I would see Him. My intuition was correct, after that day we never saw each other again. My lonely and unfulfilled days had begun.

The summer days felt like the gloom and sadness of winter no matter how hard I tried to make the days better. I couldn't help but wonder what He was doing; if he was ok. Even though we lived in a small town with so few people that running into the same people daily was normal, he and I never once crossed paths again. This was surprisingly strange. By this time my family and I had relocated to another church, however, I still had His sister as my best friend and I had gotten a little more freedom outside of the house. Yet, for some reason we never ran into each other, though He was still around. So, I managed to occupy my time with work, amongst other things which distracted me from what was now my new reality. I never stopped thinking and wandering about Him but I found ways to manage my feelings for Him which were still very strong and real. I just accepted what I couldn't change.

As my junior year in high school came, I dreaded the first day of school like most students even though my fear was of a different sort. I feared the emptiness I knew lay in wait ahead. I feared the idea of not seeing the only person who gave me purpose for even wanting to make it to school every day. I feared the idea of experiencing something new. I had grown used to being in or around His presence in some way over the years but now it was really clear that it wasn't going to happen. This to me was very hard to accept. I was able to hide my feelings well on the outside, though the inside of me was screaming with sadness.

CHAPTER FIVE – MEMORIES OF HIM

Memories are always good to have. They help us remember and reflect on the things we experience in life. Whether the memories are good or bad, they still have a way of leaving a mental foot print in our lives. Well, personally, he had made a memorable mental foot print in my life. All I had left of Him were memories and hope. Hope that we would run into one another once more.

During school I would find myself searching the hallways praying that He would show up at school for one reason or the other. After all of my praying and wishing and wandering I still never saw Him again and His sister never talked about Him. I forced my mind to forget about Him but my heart wasn't ready to follow. Of course, I received many questions from many people about how I felt now that He was gone. Little did they know each question asked was like a dagger piercing not only my heart but my soul.

    Time went by and I remembered it all just like it was yesterday that we were out on the yard at school. I remember seeing His Mom, who by the way, worked at the school. She was on the side walk and around her gathered a few people. I tried not to pay any attention; I was really trying to escape from seeing her. Seeing her was Just like seeing Him since they looked so much alike. Also, because by seeing her I knew my curiosity about Him would be aroused and I would be tempted to ask, "where is He?" "How is He doing?" and "is He still around?" These were questions I had forced myself to move on from. So, yes, I would have preferred to continue on walking in the building. Then someone called my name and said "girl have you seen this!" I turned around and said seen what?" She said "this!" In her hand there was a picture and before I could say anything, I all of a sudden got weak and didn't feel so good. I was taken back by what I was seeing. As I stood there glaring at this picture my heart sank to my knees, my eyes watered a little with sadness, and I literally became weak in the knees. I took the picture in my hands and all I could do was stare at it. Emotions ran through my body as if they were on a racetrack. I tried hard to hide my true emotions. All I could say was, "OMG!" "He's gone, He's really gone." I had in my hand a picture of Him dressed in His Air Force Uniform. He had completed His basic training in the Service. This not only felt like a shock, but a seal of fate as well. In my mind if I wasn't sure before then I was for sure and convinced now that He and I would never see one another again. As far as I knew He was on the other side of the earth with no plans on returning.

As I stood there still starring at the picture I stated "He still looks good." "But I didn't know he wanted to go into the service." I then asked his mom if I could keep the picture. She of course said yes. I was a little relieved. As much as I thought of Him, this picture would come in handy because this was a longer lasting souvenir.

My junior year in high school had come and gone and all I had left were the memories of Him. I remember asking God "why did He have to go so far away?" In my mind, He had gone away to a faraway land. A part of me was gone with Him and I didn't know if it would ever return.

During the summer after my junior year I worked as usual, but still had high hopes of Him Coming home to visit; this would be just another hope. Although, I fully understood my reality, my heart was never satisfied, but my life still had to go on. I found a job working at Pizza Hut and I also took driving lessons that summer. After passing, I now had a new challenge. If I saved up enough money, I could get a car. I was definitely up for this challenge. This would give me more freedom to move around town and be out of the house and be more independent. So, this was a big deal for me. Being able to drive around town was a big deal to all teenagers; somehow, I felt more thankful. I never would have imagined myself purchasing my own car with money I saved up, not to mention purchasing a brand-new car with no mileage. I was overjoyed and very proud of myself. This proved that I could accomplish anything I wanted in life.

In case you're wondering if I thought of Him, you would be correct. I did think of Him and How if only He was around, he might see me differently now. With the wind in my hair I must admit, I enjoyed my accomplishment and it did come with freedom to move around. Then came my Senior year of High school. Unlike during my junior year, getting into my last year of school had gotten easier. I still thought about Him and my Love never changed but I knew I had to live my life. So, I packed my feelings away in a special place inside my heart. Of course, I had a boyfriend or two during school but it wasn't like being with Him.

Then that special day arrived; it was now my graduation time. Yes, I was very overjoyed that my years of being a student at high school had come to an end. There were a lot of memories being left behind from those years. More-so, I was hopeful and full of anticipation because here was another possibility of seeing Him for this was not only my graduation, but His sister's as well. So, yes, I was very much anticipating having Him there for our graduation. He would see us both step into the New world awaiting us both. I was so certain that He would be there and once again this became my motivation. Sure, I was excited about finally becoming an adult, sure I was excited even more about the after parties I was sure to attend, but I looked forward to seeing Him and His handsome face with the dimples that could melt your heart and the smile that goes with it even more. I wanted to talk to Him and see how life was going for Him and maybe expressing my feelings to Him which still very much existed. Well, I got my disappointing answer, He was not there. For good reasons of course, He now was living far away and couldn't make it. I concluded again that maybe it just wasn't meant to be and I had no control over this anymore than I had any control over what had happened in the past that caused us to separate in the first place.

To me, all of these things became signs that I really did have to take my friend's advice. She told me that "If I Loved Him, I needed to Let Him go and if He comes back that's how I would know He's mine." With this in mind I finally just let go of the idea of him and I. I then became curious about the test of time. Just thinking how amazing it would be one day if the stars aligned and He and I would have another chance at life and Love. Just the idea of him and I learning about each other again, not as teenagers but as adults in charge of our own decisions, was nothing but pure blissfulness. But only time would tell.

CHAPTER SIX - LIFE FOR ME

We all have lived long enough and experienced enough of life to know that we can't always have what we want out of it. There are so many directions life can pull us towards. This also holds true for me. I eventually went off to college even though it wasn't my first choice. I, at first, was set to attend cosmetology school but classes somehow became filled and I couldn't get in at the time. See this is another example of how life pulls you in different directions. Instead of settling I enrolled in a junior college where I would take general studies and business. This would be the start of life on my own.

The freedom that came with this life I embraced very much. I became a free spirit. I, like most first-time college students, made the best of my time outside of my classes. I got used to my environment, then because I had classmates on my campus as well as other school campuses, I would visit them, and we hung out a lot. Eventually like most I got into the party life of college. While my classmates soon got so homesick and began traveling home on the weekends, I was enjoying my independence too much. I rarely traveled home in the beginning. Not a year later an ex boy friend of mine started attending school on the campus I visited most, we became reconnected again. Eventually this relationship would become more of a friends with benefits type of relationship. The lesson I learned then was that people change as they grow. Yet I couldn't pull myself far enough away from it. I continued to allow myself to get caught up in a cycle of we are –now we are not type of relationship and I soon learned this was not healthy. Even though I had moved on in my life and even at the young age that I was, I still wanted to find Love. It felt as if I wasn't so sure where but I could get to it.

One evening as I was at my dormitory walking across the balcony, I heard a "who is that?" being shouted from down below. I realized it was my attention they were trying to get, I shouted back "why do you want to know?" From then on, a relationship started. It turns out this person also attended the same campus I spent a lot of my time on. This would also be a life changing encounter that would be with me for the rest of my life. This person would become the father of my one and only child. After visiting one another's campuses and hanging out a lot, before we knew it the spring semester had ended and summer break was next. We were both from different places so we agreed to catch back up when the fall semester of college would begin. So, when the summer began for me, I went home. I worked multiple jobs including my family's restaurant. I would spend most of my hours here if I wasn't at my grocery store job or my fast food job, which were already set up for me by the time I came home for the summer.

One day I started feeling sick and being a very strong-willed person and all, I didn't think much of it. By this time, my cousin and a high school friend of mine worked beside me at the family restaurant. Even after witnessing them go through illnesses and finding out that they were pregnant, I really didn't think anything of my own illness. I was thinking there could be no way we would all be pregnant at the same time, being at the same job and all. I resolutely stuck to what I would now admit was a state of denial. One day out of the blues my mom asked me, "Girl, are you pregnant? You sure have been sick a lot." My honest answer to her was "No, I'm not pregnant." As indeed everything was normal with my body. There really was no way that I could be pregnant. Besides, I was working multiple jobs and always busy which could account for how I was always feeling tired. At least that's what I would tell myself. I was 20 years old. I had no idea how pregnancy symptoms came. Never mind, the thought of this happening to me at this age. I was busy working to pay my car note, insurance, and for my school wardrobe. I just couldn't possibly be pregnant now.

A few more days went by and my mother called me again. This time her words were "girl, you need to make your doctors' appointment. You are pregnant!" she sounded so sure of it too! I again said, "NO! I'm not! I'm just working so much but I will go ahead and ease your mind and make me an appointment." The day I went for my appointment came as a huge shock. Yep, she was right. I really was pregnant. I remember thinking of my cousin and my friend, and saying dang we are really all pregnant at the same time. Once I embraced the idea of being pregnant, I fully took on role of motherhood. This brought out a side of me that I never knew existed within my own self. So, instead of being sad and regretful, I found myself in love with this bundle of joy.

I couldn't believe there was a life growing inside of me. I continued to work my 3 jobs and yes, unlike a lot of others, I continued to attend college. I never once looked at my unexpected and life changing situation as a setback or a regret. I took full responsibility for the results of my own choices.

While back in college I continued to work and attend school. I changed my focus of study in school from general business to childcare development. I knew this would allow me to gain more knowledge and understanding as well as prepare me for becoming a mother. The one thing that sticks out in my mind about life is it's not what you go through that dictates the outcome, it's how well you prepare yourself for it.

As time drew nearer for me to deliver this handsome gift of life into this world, I truly felt prepared for it. I had dreamed of my gift before ever receiving it. I never expected to feel so needed and wanted by something that came gift wrapped especially for me. When I first held my gift, I remember saying "this is mine and I will take care of you no matter what. I am a mother now and I am responsible for you." Although I did find myself being a single mother, it would be safe to say that God has a way of working things out for our good. I do believe that the things that we go through in this life come as a challenge on levels that are meant to help us mature and prepare for our next level of life.

After going through unsuccessful relationships since early on, I started to understand that people come into our lives for many different reasons and for specific seasons. Some come to distract us, some to teach us, and some to simply grow us.

Regardless of who you are I do believe one or more of these types of relationships are relatable to all of us. Without life experiences we don't learn lessons, and without growth we stay stagnant and easily distracted from what our purpose in life really is. We sometimes hold onto people who are only meant to pass through our life. For me these experiences were repeated more than once. I was searching for love and I was starting to become convinced that love was evading me. Nevertheless, I was convinced that love, the true power of it and the man who embodied the definition of it, all really did exist. I was fully convinced that this was obtainable for me. So, on my search for true love I convinced myself that maybe if I lowered my standards just a little then maybe, just maybe, I would find the love I was desperately seeking.

This led to relationships that had no goals. One in particular showed me that looking for the good in a person can cause you to lose your own self and what you know to be your worth as a woman. I hadn't experienced real love, but I quickly realized that this was not what it could possibly feel like or look like. I had seen acts of Love growing up and I was certain that this was not it. After finally taking a break from my search for True Love I decided to finally focus on myself and what I wanted to accomplish for me. So, I finally decided to enroll into cosmetology school. It was always a passion of mine to become a cosmetologist. This is where I would eventually meet another level of growth. It is during this time that I would be introduced to the man who would then become the one man who was so different that I was convinced he embodied what I had been searching for.

We became united as one. However, the marriage, after a few years, would cease to exist. One of the biggest lessons learned during this time for me would be, to slow down and really pay attention to the attributes of what makes true love. After feeling the need to breath and gain independence, while still hoping to find true love, I decided to relocate to a place hours away from the life I had created over the years. My plan was to relocate and continue fulfilling my role as a single mother and as a cosmetologist full of dreams of her own. My eyes had become open to what my mind and my heart had been conceived of long before being disrupted by divorce. I had a desire to become an entrepreneur. I also knew that I would have to work to achieve this, but I was willing to do the work to achieve my desire.

In relocating I found myself once again at the mercy of searching for true love. I rekindled an old relationship that had the substance of what true love felt like. It even somewhat embodied true love, however, after a few years I realized there was a very important component in this relationship missing as well. By this time, I had started to get revelations. It's through my knowledge and understanding from previous experiences with God that I am able to recognize God's Hand in my Life. I understand from experiences of my own that

God's way is not our own way. What we may see as our plan for our lives may not be the plan God has in store. The paths we find ourselves taking on our own may lead us the long way around before we arrive at where we are truly meant to be. Speaking from personal experience, I have had many occasions in my life that I could see myself going around in what seemed like a vicious cycle of the same thing over and over. I then came to realize that the reason behind this had to be because I wasn't focusing on what I needed to learn for myself to reach my next level. I was busy doing my own thing and forgetting what my true purpose was and accepting what I was created to fulfill.

Each relationship I entered into, pushed me into my next level. It wasn't until I got close to what I understood as my mission and purpose in life that I could see and somewhat feel my true value as a woman being designed and molded by God. Right next to that feeling was a specific type of relationship with a man who would share those same values and goals. A man who not only knew the value of my worth but who also knew and understood the mission and purpose and value of himself. With all of this understanding in mind I became anxious and really started seeking answers and direction From God.

CHAPTER SEVEN - OBEDIENCE IS BETTER THAN SACRIFICE

It was at the exit of what I thought was my last door to enter, that I began to really stop and have a conversation with God. In the midst of finally having enough and surrendering my own agenda for my life, I found myself praying and pleading to God that He not only take away my desire to do my own thing but to remove what's not for me. It was at this point that I came to the realization that I was also in my own way of receiving who God had for me. The one man who embodied the true love that I had been in search of all of my life. I very much understood my own will was distracting me from my best life to come.

I have always known or felt like I knew that God had better for me, and that it wouldn't be until I moved out of my own way and gave up my own will that my Boaz would find me. I pleaded in long and deep conversations with God to not only put me on the right path in my life, but to give me another chance to finally get it right. Meaning, I knew this could not be the end and final destination He had for me. I had confessed and accepted my role in allowing myself to interfere with the plans He had for my life and I was throwing in my towel of surrender. It wasn't long before I would start receiving various messages in various ways. I remember thinking. "God you really heard me. This has got to be from you." and I prayed for signs and clarification.

One message in particular came and this message would forever be in my mind and my heart. This message that I received told me that , "I Needed To Leave And When I Get To Where I'm Going, What God Has For Me Isn't Going To Be Where I'm Going, But I Need To Leave My Comfort Zone To Get It And The Person God Has For Me Will Not Be There But I Will Find Him When I Get There And The Very Thing That Broke Me Is What Would Fix Me."

I found it very interesting how these messages along with others would come to me soon after I had made a request of qualities, I desired from the Next man I knew was in store for me. My list of qualities where very specific. One thing I was taught growing up in the church was when you pray to God, be specific in what you're asking for. God will give you the desires of your heart if you are sincere and persistent. My list would go on to include me not wanting to meet someone new. I prefer the person to be business minded like myself. I wanted the person to have children who were over a certain age. I wanted a family man, who was very comical and outgoing, handsome, willing to grow. Someone who would Love me unconditionally. Someone that I could trust and respect. Someone who had the same background growing up as I had. Someone who loves God first. Someone who isn't afraid to take the lead and knows just how to lead. I was convinced this type of man existed and was somewhere waiting me.

The message I received after this conversation with God would open my eyes even more and, in a way, made me laugh because after hearing it, I knew then that I was in Direct communication with God. The message I received was "To whom much is given, much is required." God continued by telling me that my patience will be required, my time, and Love will be required. The Miss Independent attitude will need to be let go of, because in order for this man God has for me to do his job all of these things would be required of me. I remember thinking to myself God is really hearing me. Not only is he assuring me that my prayers are not in vain, but I have to be obedient and complete the requirements set before me as a result of my requests to God. This is when I began to prepare myself to walk down this path alone with no distractions. I knew this would be the only way for me to obtain true love and happiness. I would then end my current relationship at that time and began to focus on my new journey.

After I began packing to once again relocate, I started having a feeling or sense that there was more to come in my near future. I couldn't tell in which direction it would be coming from. I felt such a dynamic magnitude of joy and peace in my spirit that I had never felt before. Knowing that I was being obedient with not only a confirmation but specific instructions with it, truly bought comfort to my soul. It was like having a fill-in-the- blank test with the answers right in front of you. Something told me that by my obedience to what God had in store for me and because of my faith I was going to receive it. I would also soon experience and learn God's timing is not our own timing. The ways in which God works are not of our ways of understanding. We may have plans for what we want to do in life but God has plans which are way better than what we could ever imagine. As you continue reading my Love Story this will become evident. I prayed for another chance to get it right; I knew what was in me to give because of my worth and I knew as well that there was a man designed specifically for me to pour all of my Love and care into. All I needed to do was play my part and be obedient and unwilling to sacrifice my happiness a bit longer no matter how crazy things may seem or how difficult they may become. I had to trust God.

CHAPTER EIGHT – HIM

Time had gone by and I was set on my mission and preparing myself to start my new life of expectation. Something happened that would change the course of my life forever. I remember being nervous and not knowing exactly what to say or how to approach my intuition. I wasn't sure of the response I would get back, or if I would get one back at all.

Years had gone by and life had changed. I wasn't even certain that I even had to correct contact. Nevertheless, I took the chance myself and left a message. Thinking to myself, "girl, you probably got the wrong number. This number probably belongs to someone else and now they know your name and your number." Either way, it was a risk I was willing to take. To my surprise the response I got back felt so welcoming and sincere. We spoke and exchanged words. As I nervously began to anticipate how I would control myself once our communication started, a part of me was rather calm in a way of certainty. However, my certainty would become an understatement to say the least. It wasn't long before our conversations of a lifetime took place. Our conversations would go on for hours nonstop. Never mind the fact that we both had work and other things to do on a daily basis. I felt like time had stopped for us. We both reminisced and laughed like we were high school kids again. Everything seemed so natural and sincere. Not one of us held back what was on our hearts and minds. Neither of us wanted to end the conversations so we didn't. We both would admit never being on the phone for these long periods of times with anyone. There was definitely something real and different about how our connection was manifesting.

Not long after our initial conversation had started, I had a dream. This dream felt so real it was hard to tell if it was even a dream at all. This would be the first of many dreams to follow. In this dream I was surrounded by many people, both family and strangers, but there was only one person who stood out. Unknowingly I was in the company of that one person who had been there the entire time and I never paid any attention to that person. We hung around the same crowd of people, but I never acknowledged this one guy who was always near me. It wasn't until one day in passing one another I turned and began expressing my feelings. It was only then that I found that my feelings were not in vain. I wasn't the only one feeling this way. Immediately we grabbed hands and were connected. From that moment on we were inseparable and the love we had for one another was undeniable. Even during times of distractions, we never lost connection as another dream would also show me. The next day is when I shared this dream. This would then be where everything I ever thought love was or even felt like would manifest itself to me. As I went on to share my dream in conversation and how blissfully in love I was with the person in my dream, I then took pleasure in finding out that I wasn't alone in my feelings. Nothing but a state of shock and happiness came over me. "Was this really happening right now?" I remember thinking to myself. It had all begun to make sense. This is where we both began to reflect and discuss how life's journey had taken a turn for the both of us and how we both had to go down our own paths. Yet we both still would come out better and stronger as individuals.

The more I shared my thoughts and the dream, the more confirmation I received. He began to reveal Himself to me. The same day I shared my dream would be the Beginning of the best days yet to come. Not only were my dreams detailed and important, but the peace of mind that came was like none that I had ever felt. After listening to me and while being so fully engaged with what I had to say His response would catch me by surprise. He would go on to say, "I assure you that you don't need to put those dreams to the side, your dreams meant something and are very detailed, your dreams are important."

We would go on with our conversation and who He was continued to reveal itself to me. I've never had the experience of meeting a man who was not only sure of who He was but was also sure of what He wanted. This man would go on to express to me His true feelings for me. Everything that I thought I knew was no longer just thoughts. I had answers and along with those answers the words "I choose You," came from this man's mouth. As I listen to the words that sounded like Music playing in the air, I remember asking God, "Is this really "HIM?" "Is this the man that you have had waiting for me all these years?" It seemed as though God had orchestrated the conversation and the words were very clear. Something told me, "girl, you can trust the words that you are hearing." Here was a man who not only knew me and my upbringing but who knew me as a person. Not only could he understand me, He knew my background, and my family. He understood me in a way only that no one else ever tried too. He had seen me and my value as a woman and took it very seriously. The things I would hear this man speak of in regard to us and our lifelong goals together and the fact that He included me in these plans left me stunned. This man came so well packaged that there was no way I wouldn't think this was from anyone but God Himself. To come not only with the guarantee of lifelong promises but a lifelong commitment to go with it. I've heard many men in my life promise many things but failed. The very fact that I knew this one came with evidence was so surreal. This brother never once said I may or I will try, yet He said, "I know that I can Benefit your life and make it better. I will do my best to make you happy and proud of me." I'm thinking to myself at the time, "wait, this is something new," I've never in my life had a man speak to me in this manner. This is very different from any man I've met.

Right as I finished my thoughts, I told Him, "you know I believe every word that your saying to me." By then something reassuring had come over me. Even though I was in amazement. He would go on to assure me that if it wasn't me then there couldn't be anyone else. This would be a familiar thought as well. I too was done with relationships that were without goals or future plans. He too had the confirmation that He was designed specifically for me. He understood that everything happens for a reason and timing was everything. It amazed me just how much we both were in tune with one another. We would go on to make sense of how our paths in life took us so far from one another, yet we would reconnect back into one another's lives when we least expected it. We both were at the same crossroad of Love, and without me even being able to anticipate His thoughts, much less before even knowing what or how he felt about me, I found out that the same prayer I was praying, He too also prayed the same specific prayer. In my mind I knew this was nothing but God. Who else could orchestrate Love in this manner? This man not only showed up, but He was prepared to Love me and every part of my very being. His knowledge and understanding of True and Genuine Love expanded far and beyond my expectations. To give you some background on this handsome, pretty complicated, cute, dimpled faced and very smooth man, He was then and still remained my motivation and my desperation all at the same time. This man still had a way of touching my soul without an invitation. He still had a way of making my heart forget its own rhythm, every part of my being still danced to the drum beat of Him except this time I wasn't afraid to show it. He still had His own signature and this brother still smelled oh so good. He still had His charismatic style. His touch was Still soft and gentle. Our Love from the beginning complimented one another. Just knowing and having evidence of knowing that Love and the Power of True Love exists was very satisfying. We both had truly come to a point in our lives where anything less than genuine Love would not do. I believe that being in one accord is very vital in a relationship. The fact that we were miles and miles apart yet never gave up on what we both knew to exist is what kept our hearts open. Most importantly, consulting God for direction is what brought him and I back together once again. This man returned to me far better than I could ever imagine. His intelligence not only as a man but as a man created and designed by God exceeds above what I have ever known. To have someone so caring and attentive yet who knows just how to lead is one of the most assuring and trusting feelings a woman could ever know. From this time forward I and the one man who could touch my heart and soothe my soul just being in His presence would go on to experience an even deeper side of our Love. Our bond together will ignite and break barriers that were within our path. We would finally be on our journey together at last as a powerful couple full of Love designed by God. It took years apart from one another to grow as individuals, little did we know we were in fact growing together in Love. I have grown to know about God's timing and ways. Being obedient in life is the guide to finding what I'm sure we all are searching for which is True Love. Love Conquers All. Love Never Fails. Most importantly, Love is patient. True Love Does Exist.

ABOUT THE AUTHOR

I come from a very small Town where I was raised with the traditional values. I am the oldest of 6 siblings. I was raised In the Church from a very young age. My family and I were very involved in the church. I lived a normal and grounded life as teenager. I was always very outgoing and outspoken as a person; more like free spirit. This allowed me to have such a fun personality most of the time. I did play sports while in High School. I loved Volleyball. I did have my select group of friends growing up in school, however, I could be a more reserved one at times. My dad was a Preacher. So, of course that made Me a P.K., which is short for Preacher's Kid. I had somewhat of a sheltered life growing up, compared to my friends. Looking back, I'm a little grateful for not having as much freedom as most did. Now I have lived and experienced life. At an early age I was taught responsibility. Some would tell me I had it easy and was spoiled. However, everything I gained as a teenager I worked for and was taught values. I began working at the age of 15. I eventually worked and saved enough to purchase my own car. I graduated High School and went on to Attend a Junior College. There I took up general Studies and Business. I became a mother and have enjoyed parenthood. I would go on to fulfil my ambition of becoming a cosmetologist. This is something I have enjoyed doing since I was younger. I enjoy perfecting my skills as a stylist as well as an entrepreneur. I have always been full of life and ambition. I was never afraid of taking chances. I became a hopeless romantic early on in my life and have never given up on True Love and being Loved.

www.ingramcontent.com/pod-product-compliance
Lightning Source LLC
Chambersburg PA
CBHW052120070526
44584CB00017B/2565